S.S.F. PUBLIC LIBRARY
West Orange
840 West Orange Avenue
South San Francisco, CA 94080

JUL 16

D0475323

To Hajo & Birgit

—Britta

Text by Patricia Hegarty
Text copyright © 2015 by Little Tiger Press
Cover art and interior illustrations copyright © 2015 by Britta Teckentrup

All rights reserved. Published in the United States by Doubleday, an imprint of Random House Children's Books,
a division of Penguin Random House LLC, New York. Originally published in the United Kingdom by Little Tiger Press in 2015.

Doubleday and the colophon are registered trademarks of Penguin Random House LLC.

Visit us on the Web! randomhousekids.com

Educators and librarians, for a variety of teaching tools, visit us at RHTeachersLibrarians.com

Library of Congress Cataloging-in-Publication Data
Teckentrup, Britta.
Tree : a peek-through picture book / by Britta Teckentrup. — First American edition.
pages ; cm
"Originally published by Little Tiger Press in the United Kingdom, in 2015."
Summary: "A book with peek-through holes that let a child view the changes in a tree throughout the four seasons" — Provided by publisher.
ISBN 978-1-101-93242-1 (hc)
1. Toy and movable books—Specimens. [1. Trees—Fiction. 2. Seasons—Fiction. 3. Toy and movable books.] I. Title.
PZ8.3.T21844Tre 2016
[E]—dc23
2015004709

MANUFACTURED IN CHINA
10 9 8 7 6 5 4 3 2
First American Edition

Random House Children's Books supports the First Amendment and celebrates the right to read.

LTK/1800/0358/0316

TREE

A Peek-Through Picture Book

DOUBLEDAY BOOKS FOR YOUNG READERS

Illustrated by
Britta Teckentrup

In the forest, all is still,
Gripped by winter's icy chill.

Squirrels scamper here and there.
Playful fox cubs sniff the air.

Birds flit through the leafy bowers.

The forest is abloom with flowers.

Snow is melting all around.
Shoots are peeping through the ground.

Owl sits watching in his tree.
No one sees as much as he.

In the trees, young bear cubs play.
Spring cannot be far away.

Blossoms fall and leaves are growing.
A gentle springtime breeze is blowing.

Birds are singing, foxes play.
Summertime is on its way.

Now summer's here, the sun is high,
Bees are humming in the sky.

Juicy apples, ripe and sweet,
Almost ready for you to eat.

On a warm midsummer's night
All the stars are shining bright.

The trees sway gently to and fro,
Shimmering in the moonlit glow.

Now it's cooler all around,
Apples tumble to the ground.

Grass is damp with morning dew.
Clouds drift across the skies of blue.

Autumn leaves turn red and gold.
Days are warm and nights grow cold.

Food is gathered and stored away,
Ready for a winter's day.

The cold north wind begins to blow.
Animals shiver. It starts to snow.

Time to shelter, find a bed,
Prepare for winter months ahead.

The forest floor is snowy white.
In his tree, Owl sits tight.

Deep midwinter's here once more—
Wise Owl has seen it all before.

It's silent now—no sounds are heard,
Not a fox cub, not a bird.

The trees are still, the snow lies deep.
All the forest has gone to sleep.

The seasons have all come and gone.

Snow has fallen, sun has shone.

Owl sees the first new buds appear,

And so begins another year. . . .